T0141428

The Octopus Game

BOOKS BY NICKY BEER

The Diminishing House
The Octopus Game

The Octopus Game
Nicky Beer

CARNEGIE MELLON UNIVERSITY PRESS
PITTSBURGH 2015

ACKNOWLEDGMENTS

Grateful acknowledgments to the editors of the journals which first published these poems, sometimes in different forms:

AGNI: "*Octopus vulgaris*," "Skin Trade," "Béla on the Shore, 1955"; *Anti-*: "Octopus Visiting Your Garden"; *Blackbird*: "Catalog Note: Artifact of Venusian Handicraft," "Restoration Portrait," "Rimbaud's Kraken"; *Connotation Press*: "Oblation"; *Fugue*: "*Ventouse Sous Verre*," "The Floating Girl"; *Gulf Coast*: "The Octopus Game," "Black Hole Itinerary"; *Indiana Review*: "Nature Film, Directed by Martin Scorsese," "Please Indicate . . ."; *Iron Horse Literary Review*: "The Burn"; *The Kenyon Review* online: "Scene 43 . . ."; *McSweeney's*: "Crackpot Arctic Octopus"; *The Nation*: "Woman in a Stanza"; *New Orleans Review*: "Annotations," "Folk Remedy," "*Pescados de Pesadillas*," "Poem"; *Pleiades*: "Unmapping Natchez"; *Poetry*: "Prairie Octopus, Awake," "Ad Hominem"; *Quarterly West*: "The God of Translation"; *The Rumpus*: "Laboratory Model"; *Sou'wester*: "Population"; *TriQuarterly*: "Frost on the Octopus"; *Waccamaw*: "Rural Spring Poem"

"*Ventouse Sous Verre*" was reprinted by *Verse Daily* on September 9, 2008. "Rural Spring Poem" was reprinted by *Verse Daily* for their May 2009 monthly feature. "Annotations," "The Floating Girl," "Frost on the Octopus," and "The God of Translation" were reprinted in *Cork Literary Review* in 2010; many thanks to Brian Turner. "Laboratory Model" was reprinted in *The Rumpus Original Poetry Anthology* (*The Rumpus*); many thanks to Brian Spears. "Rimbaud's Kraken" was reprinted in *Apocalypse Now: Poetry and Poems from the End of Days* (Upper Rubber Boot Books); many thanks to Andy McFadyen-Ketchum and Alex Lumans. "Black Hole Itinerary" was reprinted in *The New Census: An Anthology of Contemporary American Poetry* (Rescue Press); many thanks to Lauren Shapiro and Kevin González. "Nature Film, Directed by Martin Scorsese," "Population," and "Scene 43, Take 1: Interior, Sushi Restaurant" appear in *Language Lessons: Volume I* (Third Man Books); many thanks to Chet Weise. Many thanks to Sandra Yagi for the cover image.

Book design: Connie Amoroso

Library of Congress Control Number 2014943690
ISBN 978-0-88748-593-0
Copyright © 2015 by Nicky Beer
All rights reserved
Printed and bound in the United States of America

10 9 8 7 6 5 4 3 2 1

for Brian

"You embrace me, many-armed,
so hard that I grow a heart on both sides."
—Pia Tafdrup

CONTENTS

"I marvel at thee, Octopus;
If I were thou, I'd call me Us."
—Ogden Nash

"Everything became shadow and ardent aquarium."
—Rimbaud

ONE

OCTOPUS VULGARIS

The tank bubbles intermittently,
but there is no tide to sway her into grace.
Turn, and in your peripherals there's

      a sudden flex, a time-lapse lily blossoming
into your blind spot. Trebled, as if by volition,
now spread against almost the entirety
of the glass, she obscures her habitat and commands

you to the entirety of herself, her self-
      tossed parachute of cream and coral.

But no—she can never know fully the spectacle
      of her fullest extension, her underside
a mystery only glimpsed in walleyed glance,
rather than the awesome totality now

riveting you before the tank's illumined peep show,
overshadowing the static girandoles
of attendant anemone and starfish.
                     Blue-

blooded, three-hearted hedonist, she arches
      into Gehry porticoes against the thick plate
           addled by green neon, plots for the hour
when she'll heave herself out during the night

      shift, gorge herself on the neighboring scallop
habitat.

Admit it—her splay and sprawl
      has made you blush. *Just looking,*
         you think, as if such an enterprise
were safe, as if she were not
      the pupil-Pandora she is,
      who can open a jar if only
      you'll teach her.

FROST ON THE OCTOPUS

The blue-ringed octopus is one of the most poisonous
animals in the world.

She is as at the fair both circus tent
and sideshow freak within, each blue-ringed spot
an ornament and affliction intent
on advertising, in the polyglot
speech of nature, her peculiar venom
which seizes the victim first in a rush
of wonderment, freezing his limbs in some
sudden winter, all the while a weird thrush
mottles his tongue with rime, so that his first
words of love should be perfectly preserved
for this tattooed girl, this contortionist
adrift in the lonely excess of her
power, so rife with death throughout she will
at times, upon her own breath, taste its chill.

VENTOUSE SOUS VERRE

Sucker under glass

Those empty, aubergine-edged saucers, her best,
in sundry sizes,   are precisely tessellated
and creepingly uncountable.   She has laid you

a *table d'hote* of these ghost-courses against
the glass,   which is imperceptible without her,
heavy-lidded proprietress who is all raised
                                   hem and no flirt.

THE FLOATING GIRL

In Teraoka's *Wave Series* paintings the cephalopods seduce young
female divers, spread tentacles massing from corner to corner in erotic
landscapes; despite the stark Ukiyo-e inkstrokes delineating these contours
into parabolic clarity, the scenes of "loving cunnilingus" between
beast and woman create a fantastic aesthetic confusion: you can barely
differentiate the ocean waves from the indigo tattoos surging in breakers
up her body, the tide of legs engulfing her (you nearly miss the spread,
fine-haired holothurian of her sex in all the visual noise) . . . And how
can such an encounter end? Does she succumb to the enamored, oceanic
maw of her lover, a feast ravishing and ravished to be digested in the
massive pouch of some lightless Marianas? Or does she survive, but
spend moonless nights in her husband's bed longing for a confusion of
limbs unencumbered by bone? Or perhaps there is no end to this, only
an abiding Möbius strip, chiral and irreconcilable, a lesson in how ardor
ignites not in unlikeness, but unlikelihood: desire's sought-after moment
of dissolution when *What* surrenders entirely to *How*.

Please indicate the total number of sexual partners
(male or/and female): _____

Why is it that I always picture them assembled
together in my former third-grade classroom?
The one admiring the hanging gardens of mobiles
commemorating the four food groups
has only one testicle. But robust, with a textured
hue of vermilion and indigo, and heavy, as if
it trembled with the weight of its singular
responsibility. He exchanges polite smiles
with the young district chairwoman of the PTA,
whose tongue, at fifteen, had the plump,
expensive touch of toro sashimi. Both uncircumcised
men remove their hats at the same instant.
The Indian man and the Japanese woman stand
in front of the world map in topographical relief and argue
over the definition of Asia. The scholar still passionately working
on his grand unified field theory of anal sex offers his seat
to your ex. Oh. You mean didn't—? Oh. Yeah. Um.
Before trying to remember which one crucified his
frenum with a sestet of surgical steel bars, I should
probably mention that at least one person here is dead.
He's been admiring the recently unscummed aquarium,
watches its living Miró revise itself around the pietà
of a pirate's skeleton draped over a plastic treasure chest,
the flesh long rotted away past any living memory, past even grief itself.
He will not leave a single fingerprint on the glass.

ANNOTATIONS

your eyes are limpid pools

> By which I mean that they are full of bitter, stinging
> chemicals which burn the tenderest parts of the body,
> that they are necropolises for suicidal cicadas and last
> season's leaves. That they are used indolently by the very
> rich and maintained by the very poor. That a fence must
> be erected around them, or someone careless will die
> young.

all night long

> Twenty to forty-five minutes.

from heaven above; cf. *sent from above, like a turtle-dove*

> It is a sad fact that many other languages have far
> superior rhyming capabilities, particularly for the
> purposes of wooing, to our own. The French *amour* has
> the marvelous *toujours* (always) and *au secours* (help), while
> the Japanese *ai* braids with *gai* (harm) and *mai* (dance).
> Yet we are consigned to constructions which either
> betray the agnostic, or else place undue emphasis on a
> species of bird so hopelessly inbred that it has almost
> completely lost its instinctive fear of large predators, and
> thus is dangerously close to extinction.

you've broken my heart; cf. *you've ripped the still-beating heart from my chest*

> Interestingly enough, just the opposite is true: in fact,
> by means of pneumatic bolts and soldered iron and
> diverted funds intended for public benefit, you've

installed a dubious, but indestructible monument where before there was only a comfortably deserted pedestal on which every infatuated wind might be enshrined.

can't live without you

"You," in this sense, indicating the near-three-quarters of your body that is water.

THE GOD OF TRANSLATION

All the children who had been devoured
by the blue tiger *miraculously emerged from its slit*
belly whole and unharmed and even more beautiful.

The merchant's incestuous marriage
to his sister softened to a mésalliance
with a *clever witch* who suckled toads in secret.

The boy who no one heard from again
hanged himself in full view
of his mother and his sweetheart.

The venereal disease became a *dragon.*
The heart's gore in his hand became *rubies.*
The hermaphrodite became *a girl with three legs.*

BOYS IN DRESSES

Archival photograph,
Louisville Male High School Freshman Ballet, 1903

Australian Giant Cuttlefish (Sepia apama)

1.
Pubescent octet in sepia-wash, symmetrically posed
in borrowed frocks. Sausage-curl coiffure—wigs
on loan from the local Theatrical Society. A few passable
slippers in the front row, though one boy sports
his Sunday oxfords. The prima-Donald standing center's managed
to snag a proper pair of toe shoes, but stands flat-
footed, giving the lush ribbons crisscrossing his calves
a centurion gleam. His is the expression we most expect:
skeptical and detached, the barest smirk of compliance.
But it's the member of the *corps* in the upper left
that mesmerizes; while the other boys handle their skirts
as if plucking radioactive chickens, he outstretches his tulle
with a wrist meticulously arched. All of his angles—
elbow, hip, chin—are elegantly calculated.
Even his borrowed hair has an oddly sexual tousle.
He's not a handsome boy. The sharp, bladed column
of his nose draws the eye to the oblique tilt of his pout,
the unbalanced broadness of the jaw veering
into a too-narrow chin. But there's no mistaking
how the eyes smolder an invitation to anyone willing
to notice. *What you wanted doesn't matter*, they say.
What you'll want, in the end, is me.

2.
It's the sepia wash that's allowed them to see the century out,
that's kept their silver nitrate-dipped drag
from evaporating. The male *Sepia apama*, too, has occasionally

cross-dressed, though without an ounce of camp.
Here's the scene: one ample, alpha-male cuttlefish guards
his littler lady in a shallow seabed like a furious umbrella.
With gents outnumbering the dames four to one,
what else can he do? His skin glowers warnings
to the other males, stripes darkening and pulsing
the closer they approach the nuptial cave.
Sometimes they'll brawl, two Hypercolor tees
in a spin cycle. A smaller fellow drifts at a distance,
takes notes, waits for the loser to withdraw. He gives
his mantle a series of shivers, like a bedsheet snapping
leafy blotches of light on a clothesline, until he's draped
in a feminine damask of chromaphores. Flashing a dainty invitation,
he nears the big guy, whose body becomes an arched, approving
eyebrow in reply. He waves his sham-paramour in.
The back-door man becomes a front-door woman:
while the polygamist's gloating about his harem, the impostor
fucks the lady in the cave, who's more than game
to see what her new man's got up his skirt.

3.
Desire comes shaking its costume at us, laughing
at how willing we are to be duped. We've evolved for that, too:
the inclination to let pose and plumage lead us
into the undertow, the jagged, open mouth
disguised as a flower. But turn the voiceover down
to pantomime now. Let the rest be pure
choreography dipping in and out of shadows
that are live and hungry and expanding as a coral reef.
Sepia epicenes, we chase ourselves through your haze
of confounding ink. We don't want to be seen,
but seen through.

SKIN TRADE

". . . the real appeal of the showgirl
lies not in her individuality
but in the way she is multiplied
and refracted across the stage."
And so you are not known for your-
self, but by your most convenient,
refractive metaphor: an abundance
of appendage. It is your gift
of chromatic mercuriality that goes
generally unnoticed, which is,
one supposes, your intention anyway.
As the occasion dictates—hunger,
panic, slow death—you become
whatever is appropriate, a perfect
black cocktail dress of predator/prey
in your effortlessness. Even while ailing
in your convalescent tank at the National Zoo
the aptly named Marcia Frame
could observe your skin dissolve
into "half ashen and half black,
as if some imaginary line
were drawn through [your] body,"
then pale as a Victorian neurasthenic,
then a ravenous terra-cotta,
all the while assuming "flamboyant
postures." Should we take this
as a sign of great compassion
or great duplicity? Think
of the marvelous homilies and clichés
that could have been! The un-
trustworthy would be *as consistent
as an octopus's skin*; a lost

cause would be *like trying to find
a frightened octopus*; the Dalai Lama
could urge us to adopt *the empathy
of the octopus* in our encounters
with strangers. But I'm content to cross-
reference you with *scapegoat, gull, sitting duck, clay
pigeon*: in mid-century *pulpo* pulp fiction
cover art, you obligingly incarnate
whatever terror the age required.
For the 1945 summer issue
of *Planet Stories* you were a mechanical
threat, incongruously sharp-toothed
and louver-jawed as a lamprey,
a bloodied and blue arm poised
to spank the barely covered bottom
of an alienne in heels with a geisha updo.
In 1953's *Adventures into the Unknown*
the mistress of the ostentatiously, insidiously red
menace attacking the captain of the derelict
fleet hag-cackled, "**HA-HA!** Now
do you know me for what I **AM**?"
Even this hour you lurk in the news-
channel slapdash as the roiling
embrace of coastal hurricane fronts,
the inky fireclouds shrouding the steel reef
of a city skyline, the viral naiad spiraling
in the blood stream . . .
It seems this is the most salient of all
your gifts: the sheer bonelessness
of you, how you collapse
and insinuate yourself into our most private
crevasses, feeding on whatever

schools of blind and blundering alarm
the sea change offers.
To know what you are
now, we must know
what we fear first.

GIANT SQUID CAUGHT ON FILM!

You spiraled to life in greenblack and white:
the same cinematic palette by which
we first watched the sex acts of celebrities.
We loved you a little less then, having
become unforgivably visible.
Even your conciliatory gesture
of self-mutilation, that orphaned
ticker tape arm hooksnagged, helloed and good-
byed by the current, could not mollify.
We wanted a mouthless god, eyes untouched
by light. Whose judgment was not judgment but
the pulse of instinct in a cold, dim mind.
Drag the camera down. Smash its aperture.
We cannot bear to have our depths unmonstered.

TWO

SCENE 43, TAKE 1: INTERIOR, SUSHI RESTAURANT

The actor does his best to put death in his eyes.
He holds the live, fist-sized octopus before
his face and murmurs *I am sorry I am sorry*
before the cameras roll. *Action*. He stuffs
the squirming animal in his mouth. *Tear.*
Tear it a bit more, the director says. The actor jerks
the tentacles in his hand to the right
like a grotesque typewriter. *Ping!* he thinks
as he grinds his jaw. One tentacle slings itself
about his nose like a drunken friend.
He wonders if the animal, before it suffocated
in the dark acids of his belly, would catch a glimpse
of the thing that had made people want to use
his face—or rather, the lack of a thing:
that he was completely empty. Not stupid,
or cold, or cruel, but a windy place in which
everything that was not him always fit
with great ease. He was less of a man and more
of a storage space, suitable for personalities
ranging from Businessman with a Terrible Secret
to Homosexual Trapeze Artist-Detective.
He looks at the bluish knuckles of the key grip
and already knows how to play him
on his deathbed. When the actor stares at him-
self in the mirror, he thinks of snowfall
on the ocean, flattened spoons, the empty
column above the mercury in a thermometer.
He suddenly wonders if the octopus is female,
if he's doing something unseemly. Perhaps he'll be
able to play women, too, and summon the complicated
geometries of their saddest smiles. Sometimes
he worries that he'll run out of lives. The remaining

tentacles cling to his chin in a comic beard, a few
rearing up to gesture back to his face, as if to say
Him, him. He's the one, Officer.

after Park Chan-wook & Choi Min-sik

PESCADOS DE PESADILLAS

Nightmare fish

When Dalí submerged the young octopus
he'd found on the Catalan seashore
in acid, it was not
                    to watch the violent
irradiation of its skin from pearlescence
to wounded rose nor the convulsive
arabesques of its arms in the corrosive bath,
nor even for the etching he made
from its corpse so that Medusa
might be mantled with spectral,
tentacular snakes,
                    but that
he might earn from his transgression a lifetime
of dreams in which many-armed remorse
would roost upon his shoulder, lay
a chilled, reproachful catenary against his cheek
and in the instant before his ears turned
to granite he could at last hear
the soft, slightly acrid voice
pressing him for an answer
to its dark, indelible question.

NATURE FILM, DIRECTED BY MARTIN SCORSESE

Juvenile Barn Owls, Cornell Lab of Ornithology Nest Box Web Camera

Our young hero's a mixture of glamour and horror,
though Glamhorror sounds like a quaint
village in coastal Scotland famous for its
driftwood crucifixes and inbreeding. But yes,
glamour and horror, all bony yellow scrawn
and expensive-looking white down,
Hieronymous Bosch meets Ginger Rogers
(they say the feathered dress she wore
in *Top Hat* ruined dozens of takes
because of how badly it shed and gave Fred
the sneezes). His initial approach
to the dead rat was leisurely, careless even,
picking out the twangy threads of innards
one by one in a dank taffy pull, bowing
his head again and again in hungry reverence
to his feet. His body's kinked up so it appears
that his haunches are on backwards, and if
you've ever looked at a barn owl you know
that one of the more unsettling things about them
is their heart-shaped, almost human faces, likely
similar to the eloquent aspects of Circe's pig-men
moments before the autumn slaughter . . .
So the scene here is really that of a man, perhaps one
you might know, say, the myopic bartender from Sal's,
dining on a rodent nearly the size of his head
with his ass facing the wrong way. He turns
occasionally to consult with his brother juvenile
in the nest box, who's bobbing his head in time
to the tune of that universal pop standard,
"Are You Gonna Eat All That?" But while

Brother's in mid-bob, the feeding owlet
suddenly turns abruptly from him with the rat
suspended in his beak, facing the camera,
his expression unnervingly inward:
clearly, he's about to have his De Niro moment.
But not *Taxi Driver*—although wild-eyed,
skinny-ribbed Bob preening with his firearms
makes for a fine raptor in his own right—
no, it's *Goodfellas*, that great, wordless shot
of a smoke-hazed Bob at the bar, his glance skewed
slightly offscreen, dragging the cigarette, and as the slow
zoom starts, the opening chord of "Sunshine
of Your Love" kicks in like a death sentence
for the fat, mouthy gangster dangling under
Bob's gaze. We're watching the man decide it.
It's done. In those few seconds of film, Bob's already
swallowed him. Which is what
the barn owl has decided to do with the rat
carcass, yanking his head *down*, surprisingly,
to negotiate torso into beak, now stretched
aria-wide, an emphatic YES-YES-YES!
to the rapidly approaching hindquarters, the tail
riposting with a coquettish *Th-th-that's
all folks!* as it disappears into the dark maw's
aperture. The brother, in his bid for Best Supporting
Owl, has backed watchfully into the corner,
looking ready as a *Raging Bull* Pesci,
poised with towel, stool, and spit bucket,
nodding *I gotcha kid, I gotcha. Stay
in the ring.* The bird staggers back a few steps
to accommodate its newly packed gullet,
then stands there, his heavy, flurried shoulders

heaving mightily, the breastbone stretched now
as if filled with extra hearts. Chucks his beak roofward
with an expression that seems to say *Never
has anything ever been so possessed by anyone,
not even you. Yes, I'm talking to you.*

CRACKPOT ARCTIC OCTOPUS

I want to show you my blueprints.
This is where I'm going to put up the pistons,
The silver horses. I've been dreaming of
Building a giant carousel underwater, you see.

This is where I'm going. To put up the pistons
Close by the sea vents—risky, I know, but—
Building a giant carousel underwater! You see
Why it must be done. I try to keep calm,

Close by. The sea vents risk. I know but
Fucking and fighting in a green haze.
Why? It must be done. I try to keep clams
Quiet by drilling holes in their heads.

Fucking and fighting in a green haze
Will drive anyone quite crazy after a while.
Quite. By drilling holes in their heads,
The Eskimos released their demons into the sky.

Will drives anyone quite crazy. After a while
Down in the seabed it all became so clear to me.
The Eskimos released their demons. Into the sky?
Nonsense. They seeped into the ice,

Down in the seabed. It all came to me. So be clear—
This is not really what I wanted,
The nonsense they seeped into the ice,
Though I've made an amusement of it all the same.

This is not real: what I wanted,
The silver horses I've been dreaming of,

Though I've made an amusement of it. All the same,
I want to show you my blueprints.

RIMBAUD'S KRAKEN

Citizens, awake! These are not the low, mild
clouds of your usual daybreaks—behold
the slowly advancing arms of the apocalyptic
monster, already filling with a pink, sinister light!

The city is a coral reef flaunting electric crustaceans,
a lewd feast laid out for him under the heavens.
He will fiddle harshly the nude steeple of the church,
thump the opera house roof in a savage tom-tom.

His music will make the pauper priests and debutantes
run wild in the street, shucking moth-eaten cassocks
and silk-and-diamond unmentionables to careen
off one another like lascivious pinballs.

Look out, schoolteachers! He's come to suck the bones
from your bodies, to toss your slumping skins
like hobo overcoats into the gutters where you'll
spend your last breaths belching out chalk dust.

The savage urchins, those diminutive monsters
who set fire to the backs of stray dogs—
all at once they'll shriek in terror to see
their fingers turn to sardines in his thundering shadow.

The public monuments will swarm with snails,
their slime-trails a griffonage of queer divinations.
Don't bother running to the sewers to hide—
the pipes have already come alive in their catacombs, ready to strangle.

Citizens, it's all his! Your only chance now is to sprout
another quartet of limbs and clear the way as he unfurls

down the thoroughfares a hundredfold, while the paving stones squeal like spinsters under the thick, obscene banners of his arms!

BÉLA ON THE SHORE, 1955

Lighting the scene is taking
forever, and the stolen klieg's
dying. It isn't art. But living
out this penury isn't working

for him either. The mink stole, the Klee—
he'd pawned them ages ago.
Out of his pain pills and work,
he had to get back to the grind.

He pawed through the pages
of *Variety*, the *Reporter*—nothing.
His back to the wall, he ground
his teeth and said okay. Another

variation of the repertoire. Nothing
but bloodsuckers and mad scientists,
fake teeth and sadism. *Another
thirty?* Fine. He waves to the grip.

Bloody fuck. But he can't get mad. Scientist
that he is. He smiles a little. His double's
thirty-five and weaving, gripping
the flaccid arm of the giant octopus

that's miles from the double-
booked motor needed to make it move.
The flask's warm. The giant octopus
is the only sober one here, it seems.

Brackish water at his knees. *Make it move
yourself,* the director yells. *Wave the arms.*

It's only rubber. Here, it seems
like his face is breaking apart

on the direction of the swelling wavelets.
He no longer has to fake feeling ancient.
He can almost face breaking—this part,
this night, the lifeless monster in the water,

the longer it takes to feel that anything
matters. A coffin going underground.
This night is his life. A monster
one more time. And waiting.

Ah. No matter. A cough of thunder.
Some lightning. The scene. *Take
one.* There isn't any more time to wait.
Dying isn't an art—it's a living.

MARLENE DIETRICH READS RILKE ON THE LIDO, 1937

The beach is vulgar, the resort salted
like dead fish. The book is not a prop.

Strange to be called box office poison
in such a poisonous time; she imagines

the glass of a ticket booth fogged
with a sinister green mist. The latest *La Stampa*

is crumpled at her feet like a cheap towel,
a crab dozing on Stalin's mustache.

Since the studios stopped calling, she's noticed
how the headlines crawl with new dread daily:

Il Duce preening, Earhart missing,
Guernica's ruins smoking. *How elegantly*

rubble photographs, she half-thinks.
The shadow of a gull tosses

a thick X into her lap. The eagle
atop the officer's hat seemed to be

clutching the planet in its feet. He was
almost fatherly. *Nur einige kleine*

Filme. The room had no clock.
The sun tries to put its fingers in her mouth.

Her legs look strange to her in this light,
like a pair of sleek Duesenbergs,

overbuffed and idle. She shifts slightly.
Sand skitters across the page, a dry finger

underlining. *Wer jetzt kein Haus hat,*
baut sich keines mehr. She misses California,

the rampant panther tessellated
on her salon's wall. She was an officer's daughter,

he'd reminded her, a true child of the Father-
land. The teacup masked her wince.

He said that people were going to be hurt
if she stayed away too long. From a distance,

all the couples in white linen
along the shore are hasty erasures.

Someone calls her name from the boardwalk,
and she pulls her panama a little lower.

She'd tried to make her reply into screenplay,
lifted her eyebrows into the famous parabolas

that refused and promised, turned smoke
into a peek of flesh. *Möglicherweise später.*

She listens to the waves' endless collapse,
tries not to think of streets thinning to ribs,

of cities made fatherless overnight.
The world isn't like Venice, its slow

ruin—it can disappear with a click.
The light catches in her throat. *Herr: es ist Zeit.*

PHLOGISTON FOOTAGE

The lights dim. We creak in our seats.
A diver shadows the bottom of the Aegean Sea
like a ponderous yellow-footed heron
trailing a champagne wake.
Mycenaean amphorae thrust their necks
from the ashen sand, all rounding
their lips to the same vowel shape
as he plunges his glove down their gullets.
We see his fist opening rubber petals
to the camera, revealing another fist slowly
loosening itself to a walnut-sized octopus.
Nacreous and opaline, pied, rubicund,
its eyes are damn near half of it,
a livid doodle in his black hand.
Now comes the calm intervention
of the voiceover—baritone, gently professorial,
just a touch embarrassed by the excess
of its knowledge:

*One of the more unusual denizens of the coastal Mediterranean waters is the
phlogiston, commonly known to marine biologists as* Octopus phlogistonus.
*While certainly no rival to the Giant Pacific Octopus in size, nor anywhere nearly as
dangerous as the venomous Blue-Ringed Octopus, the phlogiston nevertheless possesses a
certain attribute which for the longest time could only be described as magical.*

The camera tilts down into one
of those ancient clay mouths. We gaze
into shadow for a beat longer than
seems necessary. Then: A flaw
in the underwater celluloid. A flirt
of acid on the film. A morsel of dust smuggled
into the spool. A prank of chartreuse stipples

the black, casts a fragment of ghoul-light
on tentacles scrolled backwards. Wait a moment.
Watch again. The animal takes
small bites of the darkness, releasing crumbs
of green light into the water, dozens
of sparks leaping and guttering from its underside
with mayfly brevity.

Apocryphal evidence indicates one American soldier fortunate enough to catch sight of
the phlogiston while stationed in Naples during World War II dubbed the creature The
Little Zippo—

There's no crashing grandeur here—it's the private
self-sufficiency of the animal's gesture that charms us
like a lonely whistle overheard in an empty street.
And yet, drifting in its earthenware cul-de-sac,
this diminutive marine Prometheus
could not be more dull to itself:

. . . was discovered to be thousands of bioluminescent microorganisms inhabiting the
keratin of the phlogiston's beak. The octopus scrapes the top and bottom halves of his
beak together to rid himself of the surplus buildup. This agitates the parasites, which
emit a faint greenish glow as they're released into the water. The "magic act" the
octopus performs is, in fact, nothing more than a bit of absent-minded grooming.

Which of our own human wonders may be little
more than chemical whiff,
an odd kink in the genetic helix?
The thought's enough to make us shut
our eyes, pull our ignorance a little closer,
embrace it like a mildewed doll—
dented forehead, chipped-paint stare and all.

But we're still drawn to these tenebrous theaters,
lulled by the tidewhir of the projector, detaching
our terrestrial ballast as our lungs relax to airless anemones.
Perhaps the light ruptures the darkness
so that we may better know the darkness
in the palm of our own hand.
Now they're looping a scene in night vision chartreuse,
the sparks first swarming the tentacles like spermatozoa,
then rushing the lens, spawning
with the clouds of dust in the camera's beam,
silently trickling into our laps. Look
how our hands become strange
speckled cephalopods when we try to brush them away,
the knuckles arched with primal alarm, poised to flee,
to live out their own mysteries beyond our sight.
The motor shudders. We whiff cordite.
A single celluloid tentacle whips
into the air, puddles to a glossy slither.

What remains unknown——.

THREE

HARVARD MED FIELD TRIP

Hematology goes nuts for the Rothkos,
each canvas a massive microscopic

slide, or else a blurred, centrifuged beaker
in cut-away profile. Now they cluster

around *Red and Pink on Pink*, the plasma
and leukocytes wafting into their gassy

sanguinities. The neuroscientists
loudly dissent: it seems that the artist

has simply given us the eye's last view
of a fatal stroke—a roseate window

shade scrimming gently down over the lucid
hemorrhage of its narrowing field.

A proctologist shrugs, mutters *You're all
full of shit*, strolls off to assess the Pollocks.

The guard, a vet with a flair for theatrics,
creeps across the gallery to tackle

the heart surgeon dissecting a Cornell
box (so far she's ungrafted a blind doll

from the decoupage parrots). No one's chatting
with the epidemiologist—given

Mirós, Mardens, Newmans, Martins, de Koonings,
it's the same diagnosis: *We're all doomed.*

LABORATORY MODEL

They didn't understand: I never wanted
to kill myself, just to hang in the air
a little while, my body uncommitted
to any particular surface, loose
as a starfish someone's scooped from the sea
floor and let drift back to the bottom. Only
then my head—as if the flushed and lovely
assistant in a magic trick—disappeared,
and with it my plan for getting down. But
the story had a happy ending none-
theless: they cleaned me up and screwed a silver
eye into my skull. Now I am free
to spend my hours gently swinging in and out
of the slatted light. Look at me: I can't stop smiling.

CATALOG NOTE: ARTIFACT OF VENUSIAN HANDICRAFT

Micron photograph, breast cancer cell

Stemless, you burgeon from your roots,
an amnesiac orchid, petals puzzled into collapse.

The black and white photo confers an extraterrestrial
nostalgia upon your labella and petioles;
an artifact of Venusian handicraft: primitive
gasweaving, stardust macramé.
                              You are shirred
and fine-stitched, silk-knot seed planted deep
within the sunless hour. Prune-tipped, seven-
fingered hands worked the gray into you:

you are comet ash, spacejunk shadow, the place
where color fears to go. Someone had given the nuns
from your native island a thread bobbin and a starchart;

by the time the sidereal year was out they'd covered
the harbor docks and jetties in a cataract
of parallax lace. There was no unmaking you then.

In time your sulfuric cloques and goffers smothered
the planet wholesale, the sisters long since strangled
in your threads: who needed makers once you'd learned
to spin yourself into wefthood?
                              Your new world
became bright and hot and untouchable.

Malignant frippery, even now you grow fat above our hearts.
You ornament us with retrograde satellites.

BLACK HOLE ITINERARY

Today they will offer me a dozen mirrors
and tell me to pick the one with my real face in it.

Today she'll be swimming out into the ocean to find me
and today I'll be the wave that drowns her.

Today they'll say *God has a plan for all of us*
and she'll say *God is a Cruel Motherfucker today.*

Today I'll be the bird in my head
getting fat on the sweet gray taffy of old time.

Today I will be immortal
but they'll keep setting me on fire just to check.

Today she'll summon beasts of protection
by strumming the scars on my back.

Today the spider will keep me alive for a week
before dining off of my eyes.

Today my total gravity will be monstrous.

Today they'll make me repeat her name
until its atoms split apart.

Today love will be like starlight:
when it arrives, whatever it comes from will have already collapsed.

POPULATION

After the surgery, I placed my wisdom teeth in a small blue box, and every time I lifted the lid, I felt a great surge of affection for them, those shapely, miniature Brancusis I'd grown myself. Ten days later, I discovered that four teeth were now six; two new molars, slightly smaller, and not quite as yellowed, lay in the box. After the twentieth day, ten teeth. For a while I allowed them to flourish, feeling like Mendel observing the inheritances being passed on: the tendril-esque twist in the root of the maxillary molar, an insouciant slope in the mandibular's crown. Soon they took over my small apartment—several dozen spilled out of my sugar bowl, scores of them overtopped an old boot, and countless pairs had worked their way into the back alleys between my sofa cushions. Eventually I rounded them up, and placed each in its own jar. I stacked them flush against the walls, and they rose in giant grids like a beehive. Sometimes at night I can hear, scattered from room to room, the sounds of lustful little clicks against the glass.

For Carsten René Nielsen and David Keplinger

OCTOPUS DREAM #3

1

They'd scheduled the surgery to disengage me from my parasitic twin, a headless set of arms and legs blossoming perpendicularly from our hips. When I walked she'd swayed beneath me like a willow tree. Everyone else's bodies looked lonely. Even our freckles conspired against her, marched down into the crevices of her joints to form serrated lines, like perforations in paper where half the ripping's been done for you. The scalpel buzzed like a sterile dragonfly when they placed it in my fist. The windows swelled like diastoles. And as I bore down into those hyphens, the blood dripped upwards to the ceiling, coalesced to nervy clusters of unfathomable black type.

2

—Just the latest snuff reel I'd carried with me to the surface.
No good to try and pretend that I am my waking self—look at what I become
when you subtract the world, leave me to slosh in the mind's vinegar amnion:
sadist, apologist, revisionist, hypocrite (my double? my sister?), adulteress, assassin.
Even now, in the bland ablutions of water and sunlight, her hands are reaching for my
throat.

POEM

Because they are born
without fear or understanding
of fire octopuses have been known to emerge
from tidepools where the surf had absentmindedly tossed
and stranded them and crawl directly into the glassmakers' burning
piles of soda ash that lay between them and the clamoring waves
and so at least it is innocence and not self-annihilation that moves me
back to you now even when the red creature rears before me and all my edges smolder
and what remains of me will be a charred nebula outstretched in the flux-seeded coals

THE BURN

The pink seam attaches my thumb
to my palm, ridged with frowning gray.
The pain is a loud sound. The scar could be
the beginning of a flourished name:
the claiming of my body with a contract,
or the last word in making me art.
It's the thin-lipped grin that blooms
in the wake of accidents. *I'm fine, fine.*
In the South Pacific some islanders
practiced fire-herding, letting the flames
sweep the animals onto the beach
like a great arm gesturing a gift.
What if every charred cicatrix
is the descendant of that gesture,
its species unchanged by eons
of crawling across continents?
I might hold in my tame hand
the certainty of hooves surging the dark,
the smell of singed blue feathers
climbing the air's black guywires,
the conflagration at your back
and the arrow in your throat, the last sound
the ocean endlessly swallowing itself.

OBLATION

Thousands of dead octopuses have washed up on a beach in northern Portugal. . . . They cover a 5-mile stretch of Vila Nova de Gaia beach—no reason has yet been found for their appearance. The authorities have warned the public not to eat them.

—BBC News, January 3, 2010

A poem like being stranded
on a beach: hour after hour
unsnarling the littoral for flotsam.
So what to do with this real
shore, the thousands of real
octopus corpses washed
upon it? Disembodied
dishwashers' hands: flesh
gelatinous and bismuthal,
eight fingers naked and splayed
for seagulls' alms.
But what if the shibboleth
of this pebbled charnel is not
give, but *take*? Perhaps
now the gods make
their offerings to us.
Anything can become a bier—
think of the pyramidal pile
of mice in the fridge
at the raptor rehab clinic,
each a sterile white garnished
with a little frozen flag
of blood, and how the injured
falcon absently turned one
inside out, the soundless
unzipping from whisker
to tail. Or the tangle of

maggots tumbling from
the chest of the bluebird
overturned with a hesitant stick:
your revulsion was not
of the worms, mild and pallid
tildes, but the hunger that flexed
them wildly in the air,
the prescience that your rot
would one day fatten them.
A poem like being born
behind a dead bird's heart,
eating your way into the light.

WOMAN IN A STANZA

I have seized the very edge
of my life as though
it were a grappling hook.

Once I had a body
of *indescribable lushness*.
Then a mouth that was
all obscene invitation.

Then the rush of gray
made me someone's mother,
then a rigid mockingbird,
then a mother again.

I am certain that beyond me there
are possibilities
that strain the very limits
of astonishment.

Two bodies folded
into a spasm of exclamation.
A gnarled tree wrought
from pure history.

A city, and a city,
and a city, and another
city, each one vacant and in-
violate. Yet always

this antiphon, blanched
and wholly complete.
One day I will see
the horror of my total

self: a vivisection
laid out in tidy, separate
dishes, oddly bloodless.

RESTORATION PORTRAIT

> *"Vandyke was so overburdened with commissions for portraits that*
> *he [. . .] had a number of assistants who painted the costumes of*
> *his sitters arranged on dolls, and he did not always paint even the*
> *whole of the head."*

—E. H. Gombrich, *The Story of Art*

She's practically drowning in tippets.
The windrowed stoles seize her torso
like a startled invertebrate
she'd dragged up from the seafloor
to nurse. Somewhere beneath the chemise
hides a head strangely sucking at her salt.
Her face has too many bones.

Her skin is a decadence of blue.
She has the look of someone born
to live under glass, tagged with Latin.
Something has been sketched against her elbow
to keep her from tilting out
of the frame. It is not important
whether it is a fishbowl or a tambour.
There's a bit of red in the picture where
someone's pried her stitches open.

We might peel her off in layers
and find another subject
entirely beneath the thick duff
of oil and lacquer. That sitter might even
be historical, the creature at her neck
a proper familiar after all.
There may even be scapular or habit

enough for us to see the touch of God
luminating her like a tasteful maquillage.

For now, it is impossible to say
if the likeness is good—everyone
who could have known her is dead.
A chip of white sits in the coffer
of her right eye, deliberate as a chess piece.
Her feet have been a mystery for centuries.

FOUR

UNMAPPING NATCHEZ

for Maya

Black-hinged vultures
spiral above the trees
in drugged sketches
of weather systems.

Look: the remains
of a plantation house,
four ragged columns
thrust from the earth
like a giant clawing
out of his grave.

A deer's long,
sundered jaw
wraps itself in barbed wire,
the skull overturned
somewhere in the ditch—

you must recover
it, run a fingernail
along the scribbles
where the sutures jigsaw.

This is where
sleep slips its bone
key and opens up your head.
It brings a blue
that chokes the eye.

The head is nothing
but holes
into which the world creeps.

RURAL SPRING POEM

A thrasher in the linden
cobbles an aubade from thrushes, jays,
doorslams, donkeycall, thunderclap.

The azaleas hold fistfuls of bee-sodden paper.
Out here, gunshots sound whimsical, or bored.

The new colt, still creased and kinked as an unfolded shirt,
has four comically outsized knees,
shotputs weighting him to the earth, a cool dream
above which he'd spent months
trussed and dangling.

I want to shrug out of the year,
hang it on a branch like a truant,
and float out into the deepest part of this hour,
forgetful as a fish.

I would like to wear the warm mask the sun hands me,
let my face recede into my skin like old, unstable ink.

But the sleek eggs yield blind razors
and the dogwood cannot stop
its terrible pink thoughts.

PRAIRIE OCTOPUS, AWAKE

The night's turned everything to junipers
shagged & spooked with cerulean chalk-fruit,
weird berries whiffing of Martians in rut.
I forget this isn't my universe
sometimes. Sometimes I think I was falling
most of my life to land here, a lone skirl
in the immaculate hush. In my world
I waltzed with my ink-self, my black shantung.

Owls swallow vowels in stilled trees. It's not
sleeplessness, it's fear of what the dark will
do if I don't keep a close eye on it.
Blue minutes leak from the pricked stars' prisms,
seep into the earth unchecked. Just as well—
I've hardly enough arms to gather them.

OCTOPUS VISITING YOUR GARDEN

Your fishes, violet and yellow-gilled,
bob on lengths of green twine in the light.
Bait or catch? I ask.
You cannot answer.

Your air is so very sad,
sadder still these winds, these staggering ponies,
these weak cousins to my moving waters.

It's like the touch of unbodied souls.

It's the difference between the oily surge
in your chest and the dish of blood
under the surgeon's table.

I will never understand your stones.
They seem shucked and stunned,
like they've forgotten
how to talk to one another.
They wear the faces
of senile men staring into the sun.

I love your grass, though, the way it tastes
in my arms. *Pastoral,* you say.

FOLK REMEDY

When you have done the unthinkable, the monstrous, and the shame leaches its bitter and hungry acid into your stomach, tell your secret to an octopus. He will be shocked at your traitorous indiscretions, and will clack his beak at you furiously like an almost broken typewriter. And because the guilty crave condemnation above all other things, you will feel a sweet balm rushing over the poison in your body. And with a newly lightened heart, you'll find it quite natural to turn and go, even while the octopus is still purpling gorgeously with indignation, buttonholing passing kelp and flotsam for commiseration. When he eventually dies years later your secret will emerge once more as a malignant scribble from beneath his expiring robe, but the current will quickly scramble it to brackish gibberish and none will be the wiser, and you will likely have been publicly exposed for any one of a thousand other abominations that you committed with greater and greater ease, and for which the sea is now turning the color of an open grave.

AD HOMINEM

The Poet:

> Fugitive lung, prodigal intestine—
> where's the pink crimp in my side
> where they took you out?

The Octopus:

> It must be a dull world, indeed,
> where everything appears
> to be a version or extrapolation
> of you.
>
> The birds are you.
> The springtime is you.
> Snails, hurricanes, saddles, elevators—
> everything becomes
> you.
>
> I, with a shift
> of my skin, divest my self
> to become the rock
> that shadows it.
>
> Think of when
> your reading eyes momentarily drift,
> and in that instant
>
> you see the maddening swarm of alien ciphers submerged
>   within the text
> gone before you can focus.
> That's me.

Or your dozing revelation
on the subway that you are
slowly being
digested. Me again.

I am the fever dream
in which you see your loved ones
as executioners. I am also their axe.

Friend, while you're exhausting
the end of a day
with your sad approximations,

I'm a mile deep
in the earth, vamping
my most flawless impression
of the abyss

to the wild applause of eels.

THE OCTOPUS GAME

after Vasko Popa

Two people sit side by side
And become each other's arms

They are forbidden even to scratch their own itches
Must be teachable in adjusting
The pressure from their fingernails
To rake the strange, neighboring skin

One eases sweet floes of mango
Between the other's lips
While worrying the reed
Of a proffered saxophone

It's true that one risks
Endless hours
Polishing shoes and washing dishes but

One may fire a pistol
At whomever his partner condemns
In total innocence

At last while one is nodding into sleep
The other beguiles
The dreaming arms

Into sliding his partner's
Heart out from between his ribs
And concealing it in his own chest

In retaliation the other will do
Exactly the same
When the opportunity allows

And so on until the players
Exchange stomachs heads legs

Until both walk away
Impenetrably disguised
In bodies that are at last
Perfectly obedient

NOTES

"The Floating Girl"
The quote is from an essay by John Stevenson in *Masami Teraoka: From Tradition to Technology, the Floating World Comes of Age.*

"Boys in Dresses"
Sepia-colored ink was originally derived from the ink of cuttlefish. Sepia toning is a chemical process used to preserve black-and-white photographs, which tints them brown.

"Skin Trade"
The opening lines are quoted from Erika Kinetz's "The Twilight of the Ostrich-Plumed, Rhinestone-Brassiered Las Vegas Showgirl," *The New York Times,* 8/13/2006. The quote about the octopus is from Marcia Frame's article "Octopus Swan Song," *Sea Frontiers*; 10/1994. The quote from the pulp fiction cover art is from *Adventures into the Unknown* #47; cover credit, Ken Bald, copyright American Comics Group.

"Giant Squid Caught on Film!"
"The animal—which measures roughly 25 feet (8 meters) long—was photographed 2,950 feet (900 meters) beneath the North Pacific Ocean. . . . The scientists say they snapped more than 500 images of the massive cephalopod before it broke free after snagging itself on a hook. They also recovered one of the giant squid's two longest tentacles, which severed during its struggle. The photo sequence [was] taken off Japan's Ogasawara Islands in September 2004." —James Owen, *National Geographic News*

"Scene 43, Take 1: Interior, Sushi Restaurant"
The poem is based, in part, on a scene from the 2003 movie *Oldboy*, directed by Park Chan-wook, starring Choi Min-sik.

"Béla on the Shore, 1955"
The poem is based, in part, on a scene from the 1955 movie directed by Edward D. Wood, Jr. *Bride of the Atom*, aka *Bride of the Monster.*

I've dubbed the form of this poem a "can'toum"—i.e., a failed pantoum.

"Marlene Dietrich Reads Rilke on the Lido, 1937"
German text: "Just a few little films," "Whoever has no house now, will never have one," "Perhaps later," and "Lord: it is time." The second and fourth quotes are from Stephen Mitchell's translation of Rilke's "Autumn Day," supposedly a favorite of Dietrich's.

"For those who want to enjoy something of the life of seaside luxury, I recommend hiring a deckchair and sunshade from the Hotel des Bains . . . and then read your Rilke there—as Marlene Dietrich once did. In 1937 Dietrich, no longer wishing to return to Germany from Hollywood on account of the Nazis, spent her holiday at the Hotel des Bains in the Lido. . . . Like many of her generation she had idolized [Rilke] since she was a young girl." —From Birgit Haustedt's *Rilke's Venice*, trans. Stephen Brown.

"Phlogiston Footage"
The phlogiston is an invented animal.

"Black Hole Itinerary"
Stanza 8 borrows from Neil deGrasse Tyson.

Many thanks:

to my supportive and talented colleagues in the Department of English at the University of Colorado Denver.

to Denver's lively and inspiring literary community.

to the Bread Loaf Writers' Conference, and all the dear friends met there.

to the Tennessee Aquarium, for the octopus that got this whole mess started.

to the editors and staffs of the journals that first published these poems.

to Jerry Costanzo, Cynthia Lamb, and all the folks at Carnegie Mellon University Press for their continued support of my work.

to Sandy Yagi, for her generous contribution of her limitless talent.

to my family: Beers, Talls, Colemans, Salisburys, Barkers, Davidsons, and all the familial tributaries that extend beyond.

to my brother Josh and my sister-in-law Nicole.

to my Los Angeles family, Maya, Ben, and Ziv.

to Beth, Roo, and Miles, evil pirates.

to Katie and Mike and Sam and Wyatt and Amy and Nate and Sylvie and Baxter. Far-flung, but always in my heart.

to the KC crew, Wayne, Jeanne, and little Harper.

to Jake Adam York, friend, colleague, lodestar.

to Carl Phillips, for saying, "Why stop at eight poems?"

And of course, endless thanks to my husband Brian Barker for his invaluable feedback on these poems, for being the best aquarium date ever, and for being the most inspiring creature of all.